THE GREAT ARTISTS
& THEIR WORLD
MONET

NEW
FOREST
PRESS

Publisher: Melissa Fairley
Editor: Guy Croton
Designer: Carol Davis
Production Controller: Ed Green
Production Manager: Suzy Kelly

ISBN: 978-1-84898-312-0
Library of Congress Control Number: 2010925214
Tracking number: nfp0004

North American edition copyright © TickTock Entertainment Ltd. 2010
First published in North America in 2010 by New Forest Press,
PO Box 784, Mankato, MN 56002
www.newforestpress.com

Printed in the USA
9 8 7 6 5 4 3 2 1
0 563

Every effort has been made to trace the copyright holders, and we apologize in advance for any omissions.
We would be pleased to insert the appropriate acknowledgments in any subsequent edition of this publication.

The author has asserted his right to be identified as the author of this book
in accordance with the Copyright, Design, and Patents Act, 1988.

CONTENTS

INTRODUCTION

Oscar Claude Monet was one of the founders of French Impressionism. Of all the artists who became known as the Impressionists, he remained the most faithful to the movement's aims of capturing fleeting moments, using color to depict the effects of light and of painting "en plein air." Even the name Impressionism came from the title of one of his paintings.

MOMENTS IN TIME

By painting his impressions of light, using bright colors and small brushstrokes, Monet transformed art. From early on, growing up in Le Havre on the Normandy coast, he began painting "en plein air," which means in the open air. Until then, although some artists had painted outside, the most acceptable painting procedure was in a studio. Artists often made sketches out of doors, but it was believed that finished work should be completed inside. Monet insisted that painting outside directly in front of a scene was the best way to capture the light accurately and his depictions always included far more colors than most people would assume to be there. Open air painting was never as detailed as work completed in a studio and instead of carefully defining his forms, Monet rendered everything with boldly broken brushwork.

He soon became one of the leaders of a forward-thinking group of artists, although like each of them, he developed a completely individual approach. From 1874 to 1886, he helped to organize and exhibited in five of the eight independent Impressionist exhibitions and he remained an innovator throughout his life. Even though his style changed as he grew older, he always aimed to capture spontaneous, passing moments that represent the flickering sensations of light as our eyes really see things. "I paint as a bird sings," he once told a friend. In 1874, when his painting *Impression, Sunrise* was first exhibited; viewers were horrified. The sketchy, unfinished-looking picture went against all traditional art before it and angry reviews about it appeared in the press. People thought he could not paint properly and was mocking them, showing disrespect to "real" artists. Within six years however, Impressionism had become one of the most important art movements of the late nineteenth century and has been admired by millions without interruption ever since.

Because of his commitment to the movement, with his colorful canvases of light-filled subjects, featuring momentary effects of weather, changing atmospheres and water, flowers, and figures in natural settings, Monet is often called "the father of Impressionism."

HUGE OUTPUT

Over his life, Monet produced more than 2,000 paintings and 500 drawings. His ideas and methods were revolutionary at the time and he went against family opposition to do it. His father had wanted him to join the family grocery and ship chandlery business, or at least work at something "sensible" and his aunt, who wanted to help him with his artistic ambitions, would only do so if he trained in a conventional way. But on moving to Paris when he was 19, Monet disregarded this, instead enrolling at a small studio that did not adhere to established methods of art teaching and he mixed with the avant-garde of the day. It is hard to imagine now, when we are so used to seeing images of Monet's work on everything from mouse mats to umbrellas, how shocking his pictures were at first. Yet despite the hostility toward him and scathing reviews of his work in the press, he persevered with his intentions. His family had cut him off financially and he was often so poor that he could not even afford to feed his wife and child. He endured the sneers of the public and critics and after more than twenty years of struggling, people eventually began to appreciate his work. Finally achieving fame and financial success, in 1883, he bought a house in the village of Giverny, about 45 miles (72 km) from Paris, and by 1890 he was wealthy enough to buy a plot of land next to it. Employing six gardeners, he had a garden and enormous pond built, filled with waterlilies and arched by a Japanese-style bridge. For the last thirty years of his life, he painted this untiringly, in different lights and seasons.

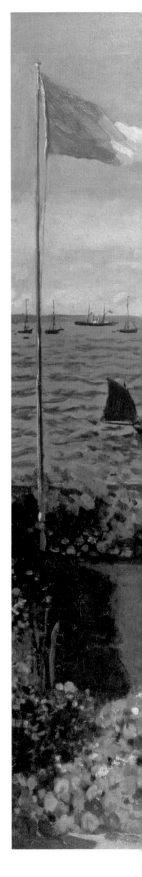

In the United States in 1870, John Rockefeller founded the Standard Oil Company.

THE WORLD IN THE 1870S

Europe was changing in the 1870s. On July 19, 1870, Napoleon III of France declared war on Prussia. The Prussian Chancellor, Otto von Bismarck, with the support of all the German states, quickly defeated Napoleon's armies. Napoleon was taken prisoner and the people of Paris suffered a siege which lasted four months during which thousands died of cold and starvation before peace was signed in January, 1871. Bismarck united the German states into a formidable new German Empire. This was to prove competition for the dominant British Empire, which in 1877 proclaimed Queen Victoria as Empress of all India. At the same time across the Atlantic, the country that was to dominate the next 100 years was growing fast. In 1870 the population of the United States was 39 million. Just 30 years later it would stand at 76 million.

CITY LIFE

Photography, still in its infancy, captured the bustling city street life. Paris was the acknowledged art capital of the world, but all major cities such as London and New York contained artists' communities. American artists such as James Whistler and Mary Cassatt were attracted to Paris to be close to the center of the revolution in art.

FRANCO-PRUSSIAN WAR

As a result of the Franco-Prussian war, France lost the provinces of Alsace, and much of Lorraine. The French were also required to pay an indemnity of five billion francs. The repercussions were graver still in Paris where many had died during the siege. The sparks of unrest which followed were quickly to ignite into a civil war raging on the streets of Paris.

圖之道鉄綜高

A RAILWAY LINE IN TAKANAWA

The impact of modernization was being felt around the world. One of the biggest changes was the advance of the railways, whose lines were spreading like tentacles across the countryside, linking cities and even countries. It was possible for the ordinary person to be mobile, to work in one place and live in another, hastening the speed of social change. In Japan the abolition of the Shoguns signaled a new era, one which was to modernize a country whose borders had until recently been closed to the rest of the world.

THE PARIS COMMUNE IN 1871

After the elections in France in February 1871, a revolutionary Republican commune was set up in Paris in opposition to the government in Versailles. The French army was sent in to recapture Paris and in the bloody street fighting that followed more than 20,000 died.

THE WORLD OF MONET

THE NOUVELLE ATHÈNES CAFÉ

Café society was very important to the artist community in Paris. It was in the cafés that they sat and talked, exchanged ideas, and often painted pictures. The Nouvelle Athènes Café became a meeting ground for the Impressionists.

Oscar Claude Monet was born on November 14, 1840, at Rue Lafitte, Paris, the son of a grocer. When he was very young, the family moved to Le Havre on the coast in order that Monet's father could join the family wholesale business. Monet's mother died when he was just 17 years old. The only early indication of his artistic leanings were his caricatures, which he sold for 10 or 20 francs each. A local artist named Eugène Boudin saw Monet's caricatures displayed in an artist's materials shop and encouraged Monet to paint. Boudin took Monet on painting excursions into the countryside. This *plein air* (open air) method of oil painting was extremely unusual for the time. Monet said: *"The fact that I've become a painter I owe to Boudin... I announced to my father that I wanted to become a painter and went off to Paris to study art."*

THE BEACH AT TROUVILLE *Eugène Boudin*

Boudin was a very influential figure in Monet's life. He met Boudin shortly after the death of his mother, and Boudin taught Monet to paint out of doors, directly in front of the subject. Boudin is reported to have told Monet that:
"everything that is painted on the spot has a strength, an intensity, and a vividness that cannot be recreated in the studio."

TERRACE AT SAINTE-ADRESSE, 1867

Monet grew up in and around Le Havre on the Normandy coast. Monet's father joined his brother-in-law's business in Le Havre. The family were prosperous and Monet often visited the family's summer house not far from the seaside town of Sainte-Adresse. Monet painted this picture when he returned there in 1867, and included his father, standing on the terrace, in a scene of such freshness that it is almost possible to feel the breeze which whips the flags.

BOULEVARD DES CAPUCINES, 1873

Monet refused to submit to the formal academic school of training when he went to Paris to study. He could not bring himself to concentrate on the studio drawings from life casts, and the official Academy view that reality should be sacrificed to the ideal. Monet quickly began to mix with friends who felt the same as he did about art, such as Auguste Renoir, and Alfred Sisley. Monet dressed in style, despite being hard up. Renoir stated that: *"He was penniless, and he wore shirts with lace cuffs."* His painting of the *Boulevard des Capucines* was made from the studio of photographer "Nadar." It is no coincidence that the picture appears similar to an early photograph, with movement captured in the blurred figures that rush by in the street below. Paris must have been an exciting place for the young Monet to live and work, contributing to what art historian E. H. Gombrich has called the "permanent revolution" in art.

FROZEN IN TIME

The influence of photography was not yet beginning to be felt, but the instantaneousness of the photograph, its ability to capture a moment in time, and its arbitrary framing of scenes were all qualities that Monet and the other Impressionist painters were seeking in their art.

THE BOATING PARTY LUNCH

Auguste Renoir

Renoir worked with Monet out of doors, painting scenes on the river Seine. Monet was to be a strong influence on Renoir, particularly Renoir's use of lighter colors in his paintings. Renoir exhibited at the first three Impressionist exhibitions but eventually his work differed from the Impressionist approach by his use of preparatory drawing and a predetermined color palette. His efforts to recreate nature using color, resulted in warm and soft pictures, often rose and pink in hue.

ST. MARTIN CANAL

Alfred Sisley

Alfred Sisley was of English descent but lived and worked just outside Paris. He devoted himself almost entirely to painting landscapes in the open-air style adopted by the Impressionists. Sisley and Pissarro, together with Monet, have come to be known as the "pure" Impressionists, which means that they strived toward naturalism by capturing the fleeting impression of light and its effects, particularly color, and tone, often on the landscape. Sisley went to stay in England during the Franco-Prussian war, painting many scenes from the suburbs surrounding London.

LORDSHIP LANE STATION

Camille Pissarro

Pissarro is the third artist, along with Monet and Sisley, who are considered to be "pure Impressionist." Pissarro was born in the West Indies and did not move to Paris until he was 24 years old. He first met Monet in 1859, and his paintings were first exhibited in the Salon des Refusés in 1863, and exhibited with the first Impressionist exhibition in 1874. He painted this picture of Lordship Lane Station in the London suburb of Dulwich in 1871. Pissarro lived in London at the time having escaped from the Franco-Prussian war that was tearing Paris apart. It is said that some 200 paintings left behind in his home in France were used by the invading German soldiers to walk across the muddy garden.

THE ART OF HIS DAY

Monet became good friends with Frédéric Bazille, who was studying art in Paris. They shared a studio in the Batignolles quarter of Paris, hence the name given to the Impressionists, the "Batignolles group." The aim of all artists, including Monet, was to exhibit work at the Salon. The Salon had existed for over 200 years and was *the* official state gallery, works being selected by the jury of the French Academy of Fine Arts. Its power, however, was fading as the rapidly changing face of art presented new and different works which did not conform to the Academy view. In 1863, the Salon des Refusés exhibited paintings that had been rejected by the jury. This alternative salon was to show more influential paintings than the official Salon, but in 1865 Monet had two works accepted by the latter. Édouard Manet came to learn of Monet when the artists' names were confused by the critics. The two artists became friends; they learned from each other, and Monet persuaded Manet to take up open-air painting.

YOUNG WOMAN DRESSED
FOR THE BALL

Berthe Morisot

The two best known female Impressionists are Berthe Morisot and Mary Cassatt. Morisot was married to Manet's brother and mixed with the Parisian artist community. She exhibited her paintings at all but one of the Impressionist exhibitions. Women were constrained by social etiquette and it was therefore impossible for them to paint in the open-air manner in the same way as their male counterparts, or deal with the working class subjects covered by the men. Instead what we see in Morisot's work are more domestic interiors and scenes depicting elegant women at leisure.

FAMILY, FRIENDS, & OTHERS

The first five years of Monet's life were spent in Paris. His family's move to Le Havre was forced by his father joining brother-in-law Jacques Lecadre's ship chandlery business. Monet's mother died in 1857, when he was 17 years old. Jacques Lecadre died the following year and his childless widow, Monet's aunt, cared for Monet until he left home a year later. Monet moved to Paris in 1859, to study painting. In 1862, he studied under art tutor Charles Gleyre. It was from 1863 onward that Monet's circle of friends grew to include some of the most influential artists of the period. He lived in the Batignolles quarter and it was in the Café Guerbois in the Rue des Batignolles, that he met with fellow artists every Monday night. Monet recollects that *"... Manet invited me to accompany him to a café where he and his friends met and talked every evening after leaving their studios. There I met Fantin-Latour, Cézanne, and Degas... the art critic Duranty, Émile Zola... I myself took along Bazille, and Renoir. Nothing could have been more stimulating than these debates with the constant clashes of opinions."*

TERRACE AT SAINTE-ADRESSE

This detail from Terrace at Sainte-Adresse (see page 9), shows Monet's father, Claude Adolphe Monet, standing on the terrace in conversation with a woman holding a yellow parasol, possibly Monet's aunt Madame Lecadre.

CAMILLE AND JEAN

Monet's first paintings to include Camille Doncieux were made in 1865, when she was 19 years old. Camille became Monet's mistress and his wife five years later. Their first son, Jean, was born in 1867, and in this double portrait of Camille and Jean, painted in 1873, he would have been about six years old. This picture gave Monet the opportunity to deal with his favorite subject—the effects of light as the sun catches the grass.

STUDIO IN THE BATIGNOLLES QUARTER

Henri Fantin-Latour

Monet first met Bazille at the studio of Charles Gleyre in 1862. Bazille and Monet were to become good friends and in 1865 they shared a studio together at 6 Rue Furstenberg in Paris. Two years later when Monet returned, penniless, to Paris after a stay in Le Havre, Bazille again offered a place for Monet to stay. Monet's hopes rested on the exhibition of his large canvas *Women in the Garden* (see page 27), but it was not accepted by the Salon and found no buyers from its place of exhibition in the shop window of the artist's supplier Latouche. Bazille bought the painting from Monet, paying for it in installments. When the Franco-Prussian war began in 1870, Bazille enlisted in the army and tragically was killed by a Prussian sniper at the age of 29. This group portrait shows Manet (seated) painting Astruc's portrait. Behind them are Zola, Maitre, Bazille, Monet, Renoir, and Otto Scholderer.

PORTRAIT OF MADAME GAUDIBERT *(detail)*, 1868

One of Monet's first patrons was the shipowner Gaudibert who was based in Le Havre. Gaudibert supported Monet from as early as 1864, but it was four years later that Monet was commissioned to paint this portrait of Madame Gaudibert.

FAMILY FORTUNES

In 1876, after several successful years as an artist, which also included several financial crises, Monet met the department store owner Ernest Hoschedé. Hoschedé was an admirer of Monet and invited him to the Hoschedé estate at the Château de Rottenburg, where Monet was given his own studio in the park. Monet was commissioned to produce four decorative paintings for the château. Camille and Jean stayed at home in Argenteuil while Monet was at the château, and it may have been during this time, when Monet and Hoschedé's wife Alice spent many an evening together, that the pair became lovers. Certainly their deep friendship started here. Hoschedé supported many of the Impressionists; but when his business ran into trouble in 1878, he was forced to sell all the paintings, causing prices and therefore the market value of their work to fall.

MONEY FROM SHOPPING

The Hoschedé department-store fortune did not last. Ernest Hoschedé was declared bankrupt in 1877, forcing him to sell his art collection. Ernest died on March 18, 1891, enabling his widow Alice to resolve the ambiguous relationship between the Hoschedé and Monet families. Alice had been Monet's mistress long before they were finally able to be married in 1892. Monet and Alice were together until Alice's death in 1911.

CAMILLE MONET ON HER DEATHBED, 1879

Monet was driven to paint the tragic scene of his wife on her deathbed. He later said: *"I caught myself watching her tragic temples, almost mechanically searching for the changing shades which death imposed upon her rigid face. Blue, yellow, gray, whatever... even before the idea had occurred to me to record her beloved features my organism was already reacting to the sensation of color..."*

A POWERFUL FRIEND (DETAIL), *Édouard Manet*

The French statesman Georges Clemenceau was a staunch supporter of Monet. Clemenceau ran a magazine entitled *La Justice* which carried many favorable reviews of Monet's paintings and even articles written by Clemenceau himself. He was instrumental in acquiring paintings by Monet for the state, especially after 1907, when he became Prime Minister of France. Clemenceau is perhaps best known for his Treaty of Versailles negotiations after World War I. This portrait was painted by Monet's friend Édouard Manet, in 1880.

JEAN MONET ASLEEP, 1868

When Monet's son, Jean, was 12 years old he inherited six more brothers and sisters. The unhappy financial fortunes of the Hoschedé family meant they were in need of a home. Ernest Hoschedé, his wife Alice, and their six children went to live with Claude and Camille Monet, their son Jean, and new-born son Michel in a house in the Rue des Mantes in Vétheuil, thirty miles outside Paris. Camille was very ill and it soon became clear she was dying. On September 5, 1879, after a long illness, Camille died. After her death Monet's sons Jean and Michel were brought up by Alice Hoschedé alongside her own children.

OPEN AIR STUDY—WOMAN
TURNED TO THE LEFT

The model for this *plein air* study, made in 1886, is thought to be Monet's step-daughter, Suzanne Hoschedé. Suzanne married the American artist Theodore Butler in 1892, but died suddenly in 1899. Monet and Suzanne's mother Alice were deeply affected by her death.

~1871~
His father dies.
Monet travels to Holland.
He receives support
from dealer Paul
Durand-Ruel

~1874~
First group
Impressionist exhibition

~1876~
Becomes friends with
Alice and Ernest
Hoschedé. Camille falls ill

~1878~
Second son Michel
is born

~1879~
Camille dies.
Fourth Impressionism
exhibition held

~1880~
Monet's first one man
exhibition is a success

~1887~
Monet's paintings
exhibited in New York
by Durand-Ruel

~1889~
A record price of 10,000
francs paid for a
Monet painting

~1892~
Marries Alice Hoschedé

~1893~
Buys land at Giverny to
develop water garden

~1911~
Alice Hoschedé dies

~1912~
Doctors diagnose
cataracts in both of
Monet's eyes

SUCCESS

Monet became famous in his own lifetime. The early years were a struggle, with money in short supply, but eventually he found patrons willing to support him. It is true to say that life was never as hard for Monet as it was for some artists, Vincent van Gogh for example, but his commitment to his art was absolute. Monet was enjoying a degree of success while in his forties, and by the time he was in his fifties his recognition was such that American artists went to Giverny to be near him, resulting in one, Theodore Butler, actually marrying into the Monet family. As a result of this widespread recognition, there exist today many records of interviews with Monet as well as articles, reviews, and family memoirs.

MADAME CLAUDE MONET
WITH HER SON JEAN IN
THE GARDEN AT ARGENTEUIL

Auguste Renoir

One of Monet's recollections described a visit by Manet in 1874 when Auguste Renoir was staying with Monet at Argenteuil. Monet's wife Camille and son Jean were sitting in the garden. All three artists set up their easels to paint the scene. *"One day, excited by the colors and light, Manet started an open air study of figures under trees. While he was working, Renoir came along. He too was captured by the mood of the moment. He asked me for palette, brush, and canvas, sat down next to Manet and started painting. Manet watched him out of the corner of his eye and now and again went over to look at his canvas... he tiptoed over to me and whispered, 'The lad has no talent. Since you are his friend tell him he might as well give up.'"*

THE GARE SAINT-LAZARE

~1914~
Eldest son Jean dies
It is suggested that Monet
paint a large Water Lily
Mural for the French
State. France enters World
War I on August 3

~1915~
Monet builds a new
studio over 75 ft (23 m)
long, to paint *Water
Lily* mural

~1918~
Armistice declared
on November 11.
Monet donates eight
paintings to the state,
chosen by Prime
Minister Clemenceau

~1919~
Monet's great friend,
Auguste Renoir, dies

~1920~
Monet is offered
membership of the
"Institute de France"—
the highest honor the
state can bestow on
artists. Monet refuses

~1923~
Regains his eyesight after
an operation on cataracts

~1925~
Burns some of his
paintings as they do
not meet his own
high expectations

~1926~
Art dealer René Gimpel
buys two paintings for
200,000 francs each.
Monet dies on
December 6

Monet knew the Gare Saint-Lazare well, as it was from here that he took the train to both Argenteuil and Le Havre. In 1877, Monet exhibited seven views of the station along with other works in a show of group Impressionist works. The story of how Monet came to paint these pictures is recounted by Jean Renoir:

"One day he said, 'I've got it! The Gare Saint-Lazare! I'll show it just as the trains are starting, with smoke from the engines so thick you can hardly see a thing. It's a fascinating sight, a dream world.' He did not of course intend to paint it from memory. He would paint it in situ so as to capture the play of sunlight on the steam rising from the locomotives."

"I'll get them to delay the train for Rouen half an hour. The light will be better then."

Renoir told him he was mad. Monet went to see the director of the Western Railway and explained that he wanted to paint either the Gare du Nord or Gare Saint-Lazare, but: *"...yours had more character."* The overawed director consented, instructing the engine driver to make steam while Monet sat and painted. Renoir finished the story by saying: *"I wouldn't have dared to paint even in front of the corner grocer!"*

WHAT DO THE PAINTINGS SAY?

THE BASIN AT ARGENTEUIL, 1872

Monet chose Argenteuil as his new home, moving to a rented house with his young family. Argenteuil was a small town which lay on the right bank of the Seine, just six miles from the main Saint-Lazare railway station in Paris. From the 1850s, the impact of the railway line was changing the provincial towns surrounding Paris. It enabled Parisians to make day trips to the rural areas, as well as enabling those living in the towns to commute to Paris. The railway also had the effect of stimulating industrial growth away from Paris and factories were beginning to be built in the first stages of urban and suburban sprawl. Monet painted many views of the Seine and countryside surrounding his new home.

This view shows families strolling along the river bank. The broken sunlight falls through the trees creating an ideal subject for Monet's brush—the perfect rural idyll. Monet would spend a very productive and happy six years at his home in Argenteuil.

In 1866 Monet painted a picture of the 19 year old Camille Doncieux. Camille became Monet's favorite model and also his mistress. Monet's father disapproved and cut off his son's allowance. At the same time, Monet suffered the blow of rejection of his big painting *Women in the Garden* by the Salon jury. In addition, Camille was pregnant and their son, Jean, was born on August 8, 1867. Fearful of the impending war with Prussia they moved to Trouville on the Normandy coast, and subsequently to London and Holland. During this period Monet's struggle to make pictures that would be accepted by the Salon and to establish his career, underwent a change. When Monet returned to Paris after the war his commitment to *en plein air* painting was greater than ever. When Boudin saw the paintings Monet brought back from his travels, he commented: *"I think he's got all the makings and is going to be the leader of our movement."*

IMPRESSION, SUNRISE, 1872

By 1872, Monet had become disenchanted with the Salon exhibition and had not entered any paintings for consideration. A group of independent painters including Monet, Renoir, Sisley, Degas, Cézanne, Pissarro, and Morisot decided to organize their own exhibiting society. On December 23, 1873, the "Société Anonyme Coopérative d'Artistes Peintres, Sculpteurs, Graveurs" was founded. An exhibition was planned for April 1874, to be held in the studios of the photographer Félix Tournachon (known as Nadar), on the Boulevard des Capucines. Monet showed nine pictures, including *Impression, Sunrise*.

THE IMPRESSIONISTS

A review of the exhibition by Louis Leroy in the satirical magazine *Le Charivari*, has become famous. He entitled the review "Exhibition of the Impressionists," and so claimed responsibility for naming the movement *Impressionism*. Leroy wrote the review in the manner of two visitors discussing the exhibition:

"What is this a painting of? Look in the catalog."
"Impression, Sunrise."
"Impression—I knew it. I was just saying to myself, if I'm impressed,
there must be an impression in there... and what freedom, what ease in the brushwork!
Wallpaper in its embryonic state is more finished than this seascape!"

The painting which caused the sensation was of a sunrise over the sea at Le Havre. It was nothing new for Monet. In this picture, as in others, he strived to create an impression of a rapidly changing scene as the orange sunlight reflected on the shimmering water.

ROUEN CATHEDRAL, PORTAL,
MORNING SUN, HARMONY IN BLUE

THE ARTIST'S VISION

THE CATHEDRAL REVOLUTION

Professionals will please excuse me, but I cannot resist the desire to establish myself as an art critic for a day. It's Claude Monet's fault. I entered Durand-Ruel's gallery to take a leisurely look again at the studies of the cathedrals of Rouen, which I had enjoyed seeing at the Giverny studio. And that's how I ended up taking that cathedral with its manifold aspects away with me, without knowing how. I can't get it out of my mind. I'm obsessed with it. I've got to talk about it. And for better or worse, I will talk."

Georges Clemenceau wrote these words in 1895, 11 years before he was elected Prime Minister of France. Clemenceau's great support for Monet helped consolidate the artist's reputation. In 1907, the year after Clemenceau was elected, the state bought one of the Rouen Cathedral paintings for the home of government in Paris, the Palais de Luxembourg.

In February 1892, Monet rented a room opposite Rouen Cathedral. He wanted to capture the atmospheric effects of light against a manmade structure rather than a natural one. Changing his canvas almost every half an hour, he carefully observed the patterns of light and shade on the stonework. He ended up producing over thirty canvases of the cathedral from three slightly different angles between 1892 and 1894, each showing a remarkable difference in color and tone. He was pleased with the pictures and included twenty in an exhibition of his recent works at Durand-Ruel's gallery in May 1895.

Rouen Cathedral

ROUEN CATHEDRAL, PORTAL, FULL
SUNLIGHT, HARMONY
IN BLUE AND GOLD

The early morning cool blues observed
in the first painting, *Morning Sun*,
Harmony in Blue, give way in this
painting to the warm golds of the full
mid-day sun. The early morning mist
has cleared to reveal the front of the
cathedral. The deep shadows throw
the building into sharp relief. Monet
painted 31 pictures of the facade of
Rouen cathedral. When he exhibited
them at Durand-Ruel's gallery in 1895,
priced at 12,000 francs, they were
a great success.

ROUEN CATHEDRAL, PORTAL, GREY
WEATHER, HARMONY IN GREY

In this third picture Monet explores the
same subject in overcast weather. There is
no direct sunlight and therefore no deep
shadow, instead the cathedral stone is
much flatter and more evenly colored.
The aims Monet had for his earlier series
of paintings on grain stacks are the same
as the aims for the cathedral series:
*"I'm plugging away at a series of different
effects but the sun goes down so quickly at
this time of year that I can't keep up with it...
the more I do, the more I see what a lot of
work it takes to render what I am looking
for, instantaneity, above all to envelop
the same light diffused everywhere."*

HOW WERE THEY MADE?

CHEVREUL'S COLOR CIRCLE

In 1839 Michel Chevreul, a Director of Dyeing at the Gobelins tapestry workshop, formulated his law of simultaneous contrast of colors. This stated something that artists had known for centuries but had never been scientifically expressed: colors placed next to each other had an effect on how each was perceived. When complementary colors are contrasted, the effect is most intense. For example, a red next to its complementary color, green, makes the red appear redder; similarly the green will appear greener.

The other fundamental complementary colors are orange and blue, and violet and yellow. Monet used this effect to its full in his painting. He said: "... color owes *its brightness to force of contrast... primary colors look brightest when they are brought into contrast with their complementaries."* Nowhere is this demonstrated better than in Monet's famous painting *Impression, Sunrise detail (above).*

The range of colors employed by artists today has hardly changed from those being used in the 1870s. The development of new color pigments and stable chemical compounds was the result of new developments in the expanding industries of France and Germany. The new colors were chiefly developed for the painting, decorating, and coach-building trades, but the artist's merchants benefited from the same discoveries. Impressionists such as Monet made full use of these colors. The invention of the collapsible tin paint tube in 1841, by the American painter John Rand, had expanded the market for pre-ground colors available over the counter. By the 1870s, it was commonplace for artists to get their paints in tin tubes from a widening selection of color pigments. Some artists still preferred to grind the pigment themselves, mixing the powders into paste with the addition of poppy oils, but most were content to do away with this chore.

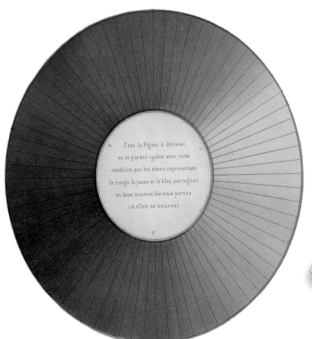

C'est la Figure 4 divisée en 72 parties égales avec cette condition que les zônes representant le rouge, le jaune et le bleu, partagent en deux moitiés les trois parties où elles se trouvent.

R

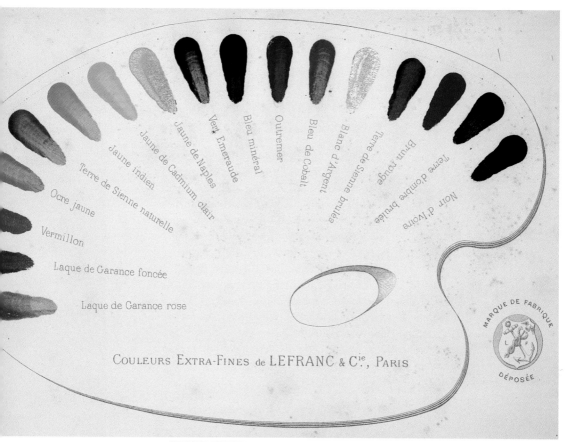

Ocre jaune

Terre de Sienne naturelle

Jaune indien

Jaune de Cadmium clair

Jaune de Naples

Vert Emeraude

Bleu minéral

Outremer

Bleu de Cobalt

Blanc d'Argent

Terre de Sienne brûlée

Brun rouge

Terre d'ombre brûlée

Noir d'Ivoire

Vermillon

Laque de Garance foncée

Laque de Garance rose

COULEURS EXTRA-FINES de LEFRANC & Cⁱᵉ, PARIS

MARQUE DE FABRIQUE

DÉPOSÉE

SAMPLE OF LEFRANC & COMPANY'S OIL PAINTS

The Impressionists embraced the new colors that were becoming available. Their obsession with capturing the changing effects of light upon their *motif* meant that they welcomed any scientific advances that could help them in their work. Lefranc sold paint to both the retail and wholesale trades, offering colors ground and unground, mixed with oils for artists. Lefranc even sold empty tin tubes, and pliers to close the tubes. Monet is known to have had colors specially hand ground for him by the color merchant Mulard in the rue Pigalle.

PORTABLE OIL PAINTS

The collapsible tube was made initially from lead or tin, but it was found that lead reacted with chemicals in some paints, so tin became the preferred material. The invention of the tube freed the artist from the studio as never before; when paints suddenly became easily transportable, artists were able to work out of doors. Another benefit was that the life of the paint was extended. The previous method of storing paint was to keep it in a small sack (made from pig's bladder), which the artist would puncture with a tack, squeezing out the paint when required; but the paint would harden quickly.

FRESH AIR IS
FASHIONABLE

THE ARTIST'S VISION
MONET'S METHODS

The Impressionists made *plein air* or open-air painting famous, but there was a tradition of painting out of doors in the 19th century. Monet's commitment to it was such, that he even dug a trench into which a large canvas could be lowered in order to work on the top portion of the picture without having to change his viewpoint. He worked directly on the canvas, without the normal preparatory drawings, and would be careful to wear dark clothing in order not to reflect light onto the canvas. The sunshade was essential. Without shade, the artist would not be able to get the right colors or tones in the glare of the sun. There were other problems. Berthe Morisot complained that: *"the moment I set up my easel more than fifty boys and girls were swarming about me...this ended in a pitched battle..."*

THE EVIDENCE

A magnified view of the painting, revealing sand stuck to the surface, is testimony to the *plein air* nature of its execution.

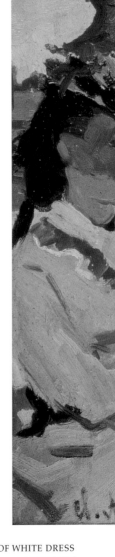

DETAIL OF WHITE DRESS

Impressionism is well known for an effect known as the *tache*, which is a colored stroke or "patch." This was an artistic development thought to have been made more widespread in the 19th century by the introduction of the flat, square brush, as opposed to the round brush. It can be seen quite clearly here in this detail.

Flat ferrule brush

THE BEACH AT TROUVILLE, 1870

The scene Monet depicts probably shows Camille, seated on the left wearing a flowered hat, with Madame Boudin in the dark dress. This was painted shortly after Monet and Camille's marriage on June 28, 1870, as it is known that they stayed at Trouville during the summer. Their son, Jean, was three years old at the time and it could be his shoe that Monet shows casually hanging on the back of the chair. When Monet painted *The Beach at Trouville*, he was preoccupied with the effects of changing light. The problems this presented could not have been greater than on the coast with sand reflecting the glare of the sun and very little in the way of shade. It was painted on the beach, and would have taken less than half an hour if we are to believe his statement, that: *"no painter could paint more than one half hour on any outdoor effect and keep the picture true to nature..."* although it is possible he returned to the same canvas later.

He had a grooved box built to take wet canvases so he could put one away and take out another, working on several at a time. In order to capture the fleeting effect of the light Monet had to work fast. *"The first painting should cover as much of the canvas as possible, no matter how roughly, so as to determine at the outset the tonality of the whole."*

The Artist's Vision
FAMOUS IMAGES

Many of Monet's paintings are familiar to us today because we are used to seeing them reproduced so many times in books and for other purposes. Impressionist paintings are probably the most popular of all; it is an easily understood art which does not ask the viewer to work hard to understand the imagery. Impressionist painting is "comfortable" to look at, its summer scenes and bright colors appealing to the eye. It is important to remember, however, that this new way of painting was challenging to its public not only in the way that it was made but also in what it showed. They had never seen such "informal" paintings before. The edge of the canvas cut off the scene in an arbitrary way, as if snapped with a camera. The subject matter included intimate domestic scenes; pictures of alcoholics; pictures of prostitutes. Never before had these subjects been considered fit for artists. When Monet set about making his paintings he was venturing into unknown territory.

LA RUE MONTORGEUIL
ON 30 JUNE 1878

In 1877, Monet had moved back to Paris, staying at an apartment on the rue d'Edimbourg. It was here that Michel, Monet's second son, was born on March 17, 1878. On June 30, 1878, a public holiday was declared for the World's Fair. The festival was a big occasion with Parisian streets decorated with flags. Monet made two street paintings. He later said: *"On 30 June, the first national holiday, I went out with my painting equipment to Rue Montorgeuil; the street was decked out with flags and the crowd was going wild. I noticed a balcony and I went up and asked permission to paint, which was granted. I came down again incognito."*

THE POPPY FIELD
AT ARGENTEUIL, 1873

Painted in 1873 when he was living in Argenteuil with Camille and their son Jean, this picture represents one of the happiest periods in Monet's life. The picture shows two pairs of figures, both comprising a woman and child. It is likely that one couple is Camille and Jean, who would have been five years old when the picture was made. Monet was relatively secure financially, although not well off. The previous year had been a success with the Parisian art dealer Paul Durand-Ruel purchasing many paintings. This, in addition to his father's inheritance, made it possible for them to rent in this rural suburb of Paris. The idyllic scene is at the heart of the appeal of Impressionist painting; a warm sunlit summer's day in a field populated with brilliant red poppies. Monet demonstrates awareness of the contrast of colors effect, placing the dabs of red in a ground of green.

WOMEN IN THE GARDEN, 1866

Édouard Manet's painting *Déjeuner sur l'Herbe* when first exhibited to the public in 1863, caused a scandal. Monet was inspired by this work and in 1865 planned a painting on the same subject, but this time to be a truthful depiction of modern life, rejecting references to art history (Manet's painting was full of art historical references) and painted with natural light *en plein air*. The picture would be huge, including 12 life size figures, and would take the 1866 Salon by storm. The picture was never finished, was partially destroyed and cut up into sections which were displayed as paintings in their own right. In 1866, Monet embarked upon an even more daring painting—*Women in the Garden*. For this picture he made no preparatory sketches. Monet worked directly on a canvas 8 ft x 6 ft 6 in (2.5 x 2 m) in size, working out of doors. It was for this picture that Monet dug a trench, lowering the painting rather than changing his own viewpoint on the subject, so concerned was he to recreate exactly what he saw. Eventually Monet conceded defeat and finished the canvas in his studio.

THE LAST OBSESSION

The water lily paintings are often considered by art historians to be the greatest paintings of Monet's career. In 1883, he rented a house at Giverny, 50 miles from Paris. Seven years later he purchased the house and shortly afterward, in 1893, purchased a meadow near the property which contained a pond fed by the Ru River, a tributary of the Seine. He employed at least six gardeners who gradually shaped the meadow into a garden of willows, irises, and water lilies specially imported from Japan. Monet painted the gardens around the house and then concentrated on the water gardens, painting them repeatedly between 1897 and his death in 1926.

MONET PAINTING WATER LILIES

This photograph shows Monet in his studio. He is holding a palette and is standing in front of one of his vast water lily canvases. In later years, Monet depended more and more on his daughter-in-law Blanche who became his continual companion. Her support was important during this time when he was diagnosed as having cataracts and was frightened of going blind. Monet finally had an operation in 1923, after losing all sight in his right eye. Monet had a large studio built in his garden, measuring 40 ft x 80 ft (12 m x 24 m), enabling him to paint his huge water lily canvases.

MORNING WITH WEEPING WILLOWS, 1916–26

The vast canvases that Monet painted toward the end of his life are considered today to be important works in the development of modern art. *Morning with Weeping Willows* is made up of three sections (the complete middle section and part of each end panel are shown here—the whole painting is shown on page 35), each measuring approximately 6 ft 6 in. x 13 ft (2m x 4m). The paintings represent not just what was in front of Monet's eyes, but equally a summary of his sensations. Monet was releasing himself from the representation of a scene in order to synthesize the recollections, impressions, and sensations that it generated. The "abstract" qualities of color and shape were the dominant consideration. Monet emphasized this by combining into a single painting, panels of different views that had been painted at different times in different conditions of light. Monet said of these pictures: *"I waited for the idea to take shape, for the groupings and composition of themes to slowly sort themselves out in my brain."* *Morning with Weeping Willows*, part of a donation to the French state at the end of World War I, was finally unveiled at the Orangerie in Paris in May 1927, five months after Monet's death.

THE WATER LILY POND, HARMONY IN GREEN, 1899

Monet had an arched wooden bridge built across the narrowest part of the pond. He also had to control the flow of the Ru River to raise the temperature of the water, in order that the imported water lilies might thrive. This caused the locals of Giverny to protest. The River Ru was used by the local population for their washing and they thought that Monet's "Japanese Garden" would pollute their water. In 1901 Monet admitted: *"These landscapes of water and reflections have become an obsession."* A gardener was employed to maintain the water lilies in such a way as to suit Monet's paintings.

**THE DRAMATIST LOUIS
FRANÇOIS NICOLAIE**

This caricature was drawn
by Monet at the age of 18.

THE AUDIENCE FOR THE PICTURES

Monet's first sales were of his caricatures. His talent for caricaturing those around him started at school, with sketches of his teachers. Monet said of caricature *"... I quickly developed a skill for it. At the age of 15, I was known all over Le Havre as a caricaturist... I charged for my portraits at 10 or 20 francs per head... had I carried on I would have been a millionaire by now."* His earliest serious patron was shipowner Gaudibert, when Monet was in his early twenties. Some patrons, such as the department store owner Ernest Hoschedé, gave invaluable financial support but the most important figure to support Monet and the Impressionist painters was art dealer Paul Durand-Ruel. Durand-Ruel bought their paintings from the early 1870s, and was responsible for showing Impressionism to an international audience in galleries in London and New York. The American patrons became very important to the commercial success of Impressionism. As the paintings became known, American critics and artists followed the fortunes of artists working in France such as Monet.

IMPRESSING AMERICA

In 1870, Monet was staying in London. It was here that he was introduced to Paul Durand-Ruel who had moved his gallery temporarily to London because of the Franco-Prussian war. Monet recalled that: *"... without Durand we would have starved like all Impressionists. We owe him everything... he risked everything more than once to support us."* In 1886, Durand-Ruel organized an exhibition of Impressionist art at the American Art Association in New York. This included 49 works by Monet and was a great success. The following year more Monet paintings were exhibited at the National Academy of Design in New York, and the Royal Society of British Artists in London.

SALES RECEIPT FOR IMPRESSIONIST PAINTINGS

This receipt dated April 12, 1893, itemizes paintings purchased by the wealthy American collector Martin Ryerson, from Paul Durand-Ruel's New York office. It includes the picture *Meules, Effet de Neige* by Monet as well as works by Lepine and Sisley. The success of Impressionism in America helped Durand-Ruel establish his New York office on prestigious 5th Avenue.

```
                    NEW YORK OFFICE,
                    315 FIFTH AVENUE (cor. 32a Street).

                              April 12th, 1893.


          M. A. Ryerson Esq.,
                       to
                Messrs.Durand-Ruel.
                -----------

    No. 341 - "L'Ile de la Grande Jatte"  - $300.
    No. 441 - "Place de la Concorde"         300.
    No. 339 - "Le Pont d'Austerlitz"         350.
    No. 440 - "Pont de Notre Dame"           300.
    No. 434 - "La Seine à St. Mammes"        350.
    No. 917 - "Aprèsmidi de Septembre"       450.
    No. 976 - "Meuls, effet de neige"      1,500.    $3,550.


              Messrs.Durand-Ruel
                     to
              M. A. Ryerson Esq.
              ---------------

                                          - $ 450.
                                            -------
    - No.2366    -      "      -      -
         Balance in favor of Messrs.Durand-Ruel  = $3,100.


  Colsmans Shipped besides.
```

A PHOTOGRAPH OF CLAUDE MONET, TAKEN AROUND 1904

GRAIN STACK, SNOW EFFECT, OVERCAST WEATHER

This painting is from the series of 15 paintings produced by Monet in 1890 and 1891, which explored the same subject time and again in different light conditions. The French title, *Meule, Effet de Neige, Temps Couvert* can be seen on the Durand-Ruel receipt with some variation.

MARTIN RYERSON WITH CLAUDE MONET

This photograph shows Ryerson with Monet in the garden at Giverny. Ryerson was an important collector of art who later became a founding trustee of the Art Institute of Chicago. Partly because of Ryerson's interest, the Art Institute of Chicago now holds one of the most important collections of Impressionist paintings in the world.

CAMILLE, OR WOMAN IN THE GREEN DRESS, 1866

In 1865, Monet painted several pictures featuring the young model, Camille Doncieux. One picture, called *Camille*, or *the Woman in the Green Dress*, attracted a great deal of attention at the Salon where it was hung. Émile Zola published an article in the daily newspaper *L'Événement* entitled "The Realists at the Salon." It read: *"I confess the painting that held my attention the longest is* Camille *by M. Monet. Here was a lively energetic canvas. I had just finished wandering through those cold and empty rooms, sick and tired of not finding any new talent, when I spotted this young woman, her long dress trailing behind, plunging into a wall as if there were a hole there. You cannot imagine what a relief it is to admire a little, when you're sick of splitting your sides with laughter and shrugging your shoulders."*

WHAT THE CRITICS SAY

The eighth and last Impressionist exhibition took place in 1886. Monet could not be persuaded to take part in this show because of the differences that had grown between him and some of his fellow artists. Degas, always quick to argue, criticized Monet's work as superficially decorative. Degas exhibited 15 pastel pictures of women bathing at the final Impressionist exhibition, which was dominated stylistically by Pointillist works such as those of Seurat and Signac. These "neo-impressionistic" paintings based on scientific color principles found no sympathy with Monet, who turned his back on the new developments to concentrate on his own individual style. In the early days of Impressionism it was the establishment in the form of the official Salon and public opinion which had criticized Monet's work. By 1886, his painting was becoming a critical and commercial success and Monet found that the new "establishment" of the Impressionist exhibitions were being challenged by the scientific objectivity of the Pointillists and the aim of Cézanne: *"...to make something solid of Impressionism."* Art historians have, over the course of the last 100 years, weighed the relative merits of the Impressionists, neo-Impressionists, and those that followed. As critical fashions change, so Monet's work becomes sometimes more, sometimes less, important and influential, than those around him.

LES ROUGO

HISTOIRE NATURELLE ET SOCIALE D

L'ŒU

ÉMI

G. CHARPEN
13,

THE MASTERPIECE

The writer Émile Zola had been very supportive of the new art of Impressionism. In 1886, however, he published a book entitled *L'Oeuvre* (The Masterpiece) which casts its leading character, artist Claude Lantier, as a failed dreamer. Several of Zola's friends thought the fictional Lantier was based upon themselves, particularly Cézanne who had until that point been a good friend of Zola. Monet wrote to fellow artist Pissarro: *"Have you read Zola's book? I am afraid it will do us a lot of harm."*

SUNDAY AFTERNOON ON THE ISLAND OF LA GRANDE JATTE

Georges Seurat

This Seurat painting, exhibited at the final Impressionism show of 1886, is typical of the Pointillist style that challenged Monet's Impressionism. Under the influence of color, theorists such as Chevreul (see pages 22 and 23), the Pointillists applied dots of color scientifically in order that colors are mixed in the viewer's eye rather than actually on the canvas.

CAMILLE, OR THE CAVERN

caricaturist Bertall

This caricature was drawn by Charles d'Arnoux who published under the pseudonym Bertall. It was published in the weekly satirical magazine *Le Journal Amusant*. Paintings hanging in the Salon exhibition were ruthlessly caricatured for the amusement of the French public regardless of the fame of the artist. The title for this caricature refers to the dark background against which the figure of Camille is depicted.

IMPROVISATION 28

Wassily Kandinsky

Kandinsky is regarded as one of the founders of abstract painting, creating "pure" abstract pictures as early as 1910. Kandinsky saw one of Monet's Grain Stack paintings (see pages 30/31), in an exhibition in Moscow in 1895 and commented: *"Suddenly, for the first time, I saw a picture. I only learned that it was a grain stack from the catalog. I couldn't recognize it myself... I vaguely realized that the object was missing from the picture... it had a power I had never even suspected."*

ART NEWS

Art News was a highly influential journal (an early copy shown left), when the famous critic and art historian Clement Greenberg wrote an article about Monet entitled *"Claude Monet: The Later Monet"* in 1957. In this critical assessment of Monet's work some 31 years after the painter's death, Greenberg concludes that Monet's vast Water Lilies paintings belonged more to *"our time and the future."* The changing fashions of art criticism are evident from Greenberg's *"dismissal of van Gogh as a great artist, but Monet's example serves better... to remind us that van Gogh may not have been a master."* In the end, it does not really matter what the critics and historians say. Judge the work as it should be judged, with your own eyes.

A LASTING IMPRESSION

Impressionism set out to achieve greater naturalism by trying to capture the effects of light and in doing so challenged the accepted conventions of the day. It not only became the leading artistic movement of its time but a commercial success as wealthy American industrialists with a taste for art became avid collectors of Monet and others. The influence of Impressionism on the succeeding generations of artists was profound, enabling them to push conventional representative art to its limits and beyond, into the abstraction which dominated the 20th century. Today Impressionism is more popular than ever, presenting, as it does, an enticing world apparently full of warm sunlit landscapes peopled by figures for whom it always appears to be a slow Sunday afternoon. Impressionist pictures are reproduced all around us; on the wall calendar; on greetings cards. It is however important to remember that this was a new art, shocking to a public who were unused to the subject matter and the way in which it was depicted.

ENCHANTED FOREST

Jackson Pollock

Greenberg writes: *"... those huge close-ups, which are the last water lilies say—to and with the radical Abstract Expressionists—that a lot of physical space is needed to develop adequately a strong pictorial idea that does not involve an illusion of deep space. The broad, daubed scribble in which the water lilies are executed says that the surface of a painting must breathe, but that its breath is to be made of the texture and body of canvas and paint, not of disembodied color."* The paintings of the Abstract Expressionist artist Jackson Pollock, owed much to the last great water lily paintings. Both the Monet and the Pollock paintings are about the artist's feelings towards colors, space, and pattern across a huge canvas.

DID YOU KNOW?
FASCINATING FACTS ABOUT THE ARTIST
AND THE TIMES IN WHICH HE WORKED

• In 1861, Monet was conscripted to serve in the French army for seven years. His family offered to pay for him to be discharged on the condition that he gave up his artistic ambitions and joined the family business, but nothing would deter him.

• Monet was sent to Algeria as part of the French cavalry in June 1861. He later said that the bright light, intense colors, and exotic culture influenced his painting for the rest of his life.

• Within two years of serving in the army, Monet contracted typhoid fever and was sent home to recover. His aunt paid for him to leave the army on the understanding that he would train at an official art school instead.

• Until he went into the army, Monet was known by his first name of Oscar, but from the time he returned and for the rest of his life, he used his middle name Claude.

• When Monet lived in London during the Franco-Prussian War, he and Pissarro studied the work of the English landscapists. At the time, he said he admired the work, especially paintings by J. M. W. Turner. He later denied

this, but his paintings show many similarities with Turner's representations of light and atmosphere.

• Subjects like railway stations and bridges were considered ugly and unsuitable as art subjects at the time, so when Monet painted these themes of modernity, people thought he was not a serious artist.

• Monet often sailed along the River Seine in his studio boat, painting the views around him.

• He had a thorough knowledge of color theories and although viewers of his work thought he was slapdash, all the marks he made and the colors he used were chosen and placed carefully.

• The surfaces of Monet's paintings are often highly textured with thick paint, another feature that went against accepted ideals of painting.

• He rarely used black but when he did, he seldom blended it with other colors to make them darker. Instead he mixed complementary colors to create darker tones.

• He was in England for Queen Victoria's funeral, which he watched and described as a "unique spectacle."

• He painted his final, huge canvases of his lily pond as a gift for the French nation. He began working on them just before the outbreak of the First World War and continued until the day of his death in December 1926, sadly, dying before he could deliver them.

• Toward the end of his life, Monet was almost blind but he carried on painting huge, brightly colored canvases. He also became increasingly fascinated by textures and explored ways of recreating the textures of nature with oil paint.

• Monet influenced many artists and art movements that followed him, including Post-Impressionism, Abstract Expressionism, Fauvism, and Color Field painting.

• Unlike most artists before him, Monet made his brushstrokes show on the canvas, which also went against accepted conventions. Visible brushstrokes showed an artist's personality—and the art authorities believed that this showed arrogance!

• Instead of waiting for each layer of paint to dry, Monet painted while his previous paint layers were still wet. This produced softer edges and more exciting blends of color.

• An editor once visited Monet to interview him and asked to see the studio. Monet gestured to the surrounding countryside and said "This is my studio!"

• The winter of 1879 to 1880 was bitter, with temperatures dropping to -25°C. The River Seine froze so thickly that it could be crossed on foot. Despite the cold, Monet set up his easel outside and painted the icy scenes before him

• *The Poplars* were one of Monet's series paintings, where he painted the same subject over and again in different lights. The line of trees was going to be felled for lumber, so Monet paid for them to be left so he could continue painting them.

• Monet was fascinated by England: he liked English breakfasts, English wool suits, English dinner parties, and the effects of London fog. In 1899, 1900, and 1901, he spent time in London, painting foggy views.

SUMMARY TIMELINE OF
THE ARTIST & HIS CONTEMPORARIES

THE LIFE OF MONET

~1840~

Rodin and Zola are born
in the same year as Monet;
Queen Victoria marries
her cousin Albert

~1848~

Revolutions occur across
Europe, changing the
ways that some countries
are governed; Louis
Comfort Tiffany and
Paul Gauguin are born

~1850~

Levi Strauss makes
his first blue jeans

~1855~

The first Exhibition
Universelle is held in
Paris, displaying French
technological and economic
progress; Pissarro arrives in
Paris from the West Indies

~1856~

Monet sells his caricatures
from Gravier's, a shop
in Le Havre

~1858~

There is an assassination
attempt on Napoleon III;
Macy's department store
opens in New York; Charles
Frederick Worth opens the first
haute couture house in Paris;
Monet's first oil painting is
exhibited in Le Havre

~1862~

Monet, Bazille, Renoir,
and Sisley meet at
Gleyre's studio in Paris

~1863~

Boudin paints *The Beach
at Trouville;* at the Salon des
Refusés, Monet sees Manet's
Le Déjeuner sur l'Herbe and
is inspired to paint in the
Forest of Fontainebleau

~1865~

Monet submits work to the
Paris Salon; in America, slavery
is abolished as the Civil War
ends after four years

~1867~

Another Exposition
Universelle is held in Paris;
Monet moves into his aunt's
house at Sainte-Adresse

~1868~

At an exhibition in Le Havre
Monet is awarded a silver
medal, he moves to Etretat and

paints Madame Gaudibert's
portrait and *Jean Monet Asleep*
among many other works

~1870~

Escaping from the Franco-
Prussian War, in London,
Monet meets Pissarro and the
art dealer Durand-Ruel

~1871~

Pissarro paints *Lordship Lane
Station;* Monet and his family
return to France via Holland
and settle in Argenteuil; Baron
Haussmann begins
modernizing Paris

~1872~

Sisley paints *The Saint Martin
Canal;* Monet paints *Impression,
Sunrise* and works on his
studio boat, Durand-Ruel buys
twenty-nine of his paintings

~1873~

The rival cities of Buda and
Pest unite to form the capital of
Hungary; Monet paints *The
Poppy Field at Argenteuil,
Camille and Jean* and

The Boulevard des Capucines
among many others

~1874~
Monet exhibits twelve works
in the first Impressionist
exhibition; Levi Strauss and
Jacob Davis receive a U.S.
patent for blue jeans
with copper rivets

~1876~
The second Impressionist
exhibition is held, Monet
exhibits eighteen works and
begins his *Gare Saint-Lazare*
series; the telephone is
invented by Alexander
Graham Bell

~1878~
Another Universelle
Exhibition opens in Paris;
Monet moves to Vétheuil, he
paints *La rue Montorgueil,
Festival of 30 June*

~1879~
Morisot paints *Young
Woman Dressed for the Ball*;
Thomas Edison demonstrates
the electric light; the
Chicago Art Institute
is founded; Monet exhibits
twenty-nine works in
the fourth Impressionist
exhibition five months
before Camille dies

~1880~
Monet does not take part
in the fifth Impressionist
exhibition, but has his first
solo show and work accepted

at the Salon; the German
painters Kirchner and
Marc and American sculptor
Epstein are born

~1881~
Renoir paints *The Luncheon
of the Boating Party*;
Picasso is born

~1883~
Manet and Gustave Doré die;
Monet and Renoir visit
Cézanne in Aix-en-Provence;
Monet moves to Giverny

~1884~
Monet paints on the
Italian Riviera; he brightens his
palette and produces six
paintings a day

~1885~
Donated by France, the
Statue of Liberty arrives in
New York1886 Durand-Ruel
holds an Impressionist
exhibition in New York,
the catalog confuses Monet
with Manet; Monet does not
exhibit in the eighth and final
Impressionist exhibition,
but sends eight works
to an exhibition in Brussels

~1889~
Commemorating the French
Revolution, the Eiffel Tower
opens; the Wall Street Journal
begins publishing; Van Gogh
paints *Starry Night*; Monet and
Rodin share an exhibition

~1895~
Monet paints in Norway, on his
return, fifty of his works are
exhibited in Paris; x-rays are
discovered, the Lumière brothers
develop a motion picture camera
and Guglielmo Marconi sends
the first radio signal; Berthe
Morisot dies

~1901~
Monet visits London for the third
consecutive year and witnesses
Queen Victoria's funeral;
Impressionist exhibitions are
held in Berlin and London;
Picasso begins
his blue period

~1908~
Monet's eyesight deteriorates;
he and Alice spend two months
in Venice; the first Model
"T" Ford goes on sale

~1918~
The Russian royal family is
murdered; World War I ends;
Monet can only distinguish
colors by paint tube labels—but
he completes eight huge water
lily paintings

~1926~
Mary Cassatt dies in the
same year as Monet

WHAT DID HE SAY ?

Here are some of the things that Monet said:

• "My garden is my most beautiful masterpiece"

• "I can only draw what I see"

• "Color is my day-long obsession, joy, and torment"

• "I perhaps owe having become a painter to flowers"

• "No one is an artist unless he carries his picture in his head before painting it, and is sure of his method and composition"

• "To paint the sea really well, you need to look at it every hour of every day in the same place so that you can understand its way in that particular spot and that is why I am working on the same motifs over and over again"

• "For me, a landscape does not exist in its own right, since its appearance changes at every moment— but the surrounding atmosphere brings it to life— the light and the air which vary continually. For me, it is only the surrounding atmosphere which gives subjects their true value"

• "I have made tremendous efforts to work in a darker register and express the sinister and tragic quality of the place, given my natural tendency to work in light and pale tones"

• "The Thames was all gold...it was beautiful, so fine that I began working in a frenzy, following the sun and its reflections on the water"

• "The only merit I have is to have painted directly from nature with the aim of conveying my impressions in front of the most fugitive effects"

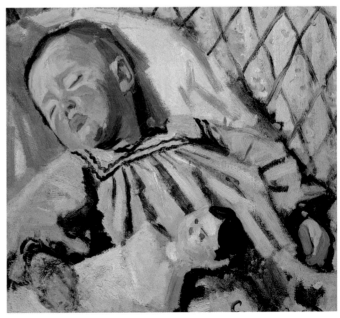

A WORK IN CLOSE-UP

La Grenouillère was a riverside bathing and boating resort with a floating restaurant not far from Paris, popular with weekend visitors during the second half of the nineteenth century. In 1869, Monet and Renoir painted there together. Both fascinated by the water, reflections, and colors, they produced several different views of the place.

Monet's paint is thick and the brushwork energetic as he painted quickly outside to capture the afternoon light.

He created the impression of overhanging trees with dark green marks, speckled with lighter patches.

For this painting, Monet used lead white, chrome yellow, lemon yellow, vermilion, cobalt violet, Prussian blue, cobalt blue, emerald green, viridian green, and chrome green.

White undercoat (primer) makes the paint appear brighter. In many places, Monet applied paint straight from the tube without blending.

Long unbroken brushstrokes outline the boats, short horizontal dashes indicate reflections, and smaller patches represent figures. The varied marks also help to suggest different textures.

Monet has combined slurred wet-in-wet mixtures of paint with wet paint over dry.

By placing complementary colors together like red and green, the painting appears fresh and bright.

Although the composition seems accidental, it was carefully planned. The horizontal duckboard cuts across the picture almost exactly halfway. An unconventional composition, Monet did this to emphasize the patterns of light and dark tones in the top and bottom halves of the canvas.

Bathing at La Grenouillère, 1869, oil on canvas, 28 x 36 in/73 x 92 cm, *The National Gallery, London, UK*

WHERE TO SEE THIS ARTIST'S WORKS IN THE USA

There are many places in the USA with works by Monet. It's always a good idea to check before visiting to make sure that a work you wish to see is on display.

The Art Institute
of Chicago,
Chicago, Illinois
(www.artic.edu)

The Detroit Institute
of Arts,
Detroit, Michigan
(www.dia.org)

Fine Arts Museums
of San Francisco,
San Francisco, California
(www.famsf.org)

The Guggenheim Museum,
New York
(www.guggenheim.org)

J. Paul Getty Museum,
Los Angeles, California
(www.getty.edu)

Museum of Fine Arts,
Houston, Texas
(www.mfah.org)

Norton Simon Museum,
Pasadena, California
(www.nortonsimon.org)

Museum of Fine Arts,
Boston, Massachusetts
(www.mfa.org)

Museum of Modern Art,
New York (www.moma.org)

The National Gallery of Art,
Washington D.C.
(www.nga.gov)

Nelson-Atkins
Museum of Art,
Kansas City, Missouri
(www.nelson-atkins.org)

Albright-Knox Art Gallery,
Buffalo, New York
(www.albrightknox.org)

Allen Memorial Art
Museum at Oberlin
College,
Ohio
(www.oberlin.edu)

Carnegie Museum of Art,
Pittsburgh, Pennsylvania
(www.cmoa.org)

The Cleveland Museum
of Art,
Cleveland, Ohio
(www.clevelandart.org)

Columbus Museum of Art,
Ohio
(www.columbusmuseum.org)

Five College Museums,
Massachusetts
(museums.fivecolleges.edu)

Frick Collection,
New York City, New York
(collections.frick.org)

Hill-Stead Museum,
Farmington, Connecticut
(www.hillstead.org)

Harvard University
Art Museums,
Massachusetts
(www.artmuseums.
harvard.edu)

Indianapolis Museum
of Art,
Indianapolis, Indiana
(www.imamuseum.org)

Kimbell Art Museum,
Fort Worth, Texas
(www.kimbellart.org)

Memorial Art Gallery
of the University
of Rochester,
New York
(magart.rochester.edu)

Milwaukee Art Museum,
Wisconsin
(www.mam.org)

Minneapolis Institute
of Art,
Minneapolis, Minnesota
(www.artsmia.org)

Philadelphia Museum
of Art,
Pennsylvania
(www.philamuseum.org)

Saint Louis Art Museum,
St. Louis, Missouri
(stlouis.art.museum)

Smith College
Museum of Art,
Northampton,
Massachusetts
(www.smith.edu)

Worcester Art Museum,
Worcester, Massachusetts
(www.worcesterart.org)

Wadsworth Museum
of Art,
Hartford, Connecticut
(www.wadsworthatheneum.
org)

WHERE TO SEE THIS ARTIST'S WORKS IN THE REST OF THE WORLD

There are many places in which to see works by Monet. Listed here are a few of them. Always check before visiting, to make sure that the work you wish to see is on display.

The State Hermitage Museum,
St. Petersburg, Russia
(www.hermitagemuseum.org)

The Fitzwilliam Museum,
Cambridge, England
(www.fitzmuseum.cam.ac.uk)

Louvre Museum,
Paris, France
(www.louvre.fr)

Musée d'Orsay,
Paris, France
(www.musee-orsay.fr)

Musée Marmottan,
Paris, France
(www.marmottan.com)

National Gallery,
London, England
(www.nationalgallery.org.uk)

National Galleries
of Scotland,
Edinburgh, Scotland
(www.nationalgalleries.org)

Neue Pinakothek,
Munich, Germany
(www.pinakothek.de)

Ashmolean Museum,
Oxford, England
(www.ashmolean.org)

The Barber Institute
of Fine Arts,
Birmingham, England
(www.barber.org.uk)

Beyeler Foundation
Collection,
Basel, Switzerland
(www.beyeler.com)

E. G. Bürhle Collection,
Zürich, Switzerland
(www.buehrle.ch)

Fondation Bemberg
Museum,
Toulouse, France
(www.fondation-bemberg.fr)

Kelvingrove Art Gallery
and Museum,
Glasgow, Scotland
(www.glasgowmuseums.com)

Kunstmuseum Basel,
Basel, Switzerland
(www.kunstmuseumbasel.ch)

Kunstmuseum Winterthur,
Winterthur, Switzerland
(www.kmw.ch)

Musée de l'Orangerie,
Paris, France
(www.musee-orangerie.fr)

Musée des Beaux-
Arts de Rouen,
Rouen, France
(www.rouen-musees.com)

Musées de Lorraine,
Lorraine, France
(www.fram-
museesdelorraine.org)

Museum Boijmans
Van Beuningen,
Rotterdam,
The Netherlands
(www.boijmans.nl)

Museu Calouste
Gulbenkian,
Lisbon, Portugal
(museu.gulbenkian.pt)

Museo Nacional de
Bellas Artes,
Buenos Aires, Argentina
(www.mnba.org.ar)

National Gallery
of Victoria,
Victoria, Australia
(www.ngv.vic.gov.au)

National Museum
of Western Art,
Tokyo, Japan
(www.tnm.go.jp)

National Museum and
Gallery of Wales,
Cardiff, Wales
(www.museumwales.ac.uk)

The National Museum
of Art of Romania,
Bucharest, Romania
(www.mnar.arts.ro)

Walker Art Gallery,
Liverpool, England
(www.liverpool
museums.org.uk)

New Carlsberg Glyptotek,
Copenhagen, Denmark
(www.glyptoteket.dk)

Oskar Reinhart Collection,
Winterthur, Switzerland
(www.roemerholz.ch)

Österreichische Galerie
Belvedere,
Vienna, Austria
(www.belvedere.at)

Pushkin State Museum
of Fine Arts,
Moscow, Russia
(www.museum.ru)

Staatsgalerie,
Stuttgart, Germany
(www.staatsgalerie.de)

Tate Gallery,
London, England
(www.tate.org.uk)

Museo Thyssen-
Bornemisza,
Madrid, Spain
(www.museothyssen.org)

Van Gogh Museum,
Amsterdam,
The Netherlands
(www.vangoghmuseum.nl)

Von der Heydt-Museum,
Wuppertal, Germany
(www.von-der-heydt-
museum.de)

FURTHER READING & WEBSITES

BOOKS

Monet's Impressions,
Metropolitan Museum
of Art,
Chronicle Books, 2009

Claude Monet
(Artists in their World),
Susie Hodge,
Franklin Watts, 2005

Claude Monet
(The Life and Work of),
Sean Connolly,
Heinemann Library, 2007

The Magical Garden
of Claude Monet,
Laurence Anholt,
Frances Lincoln Publishers,
2007

Claude Monet: The
Magician of Colour
(Adventures in Art),
Stephan Koja and
Katja Miksovsky,
Prestel, 1997

Claude Monet: Sunshine
and Waterlilies,
True Kelley,
Grosset and Dunlap, 2001

Who was Claude Monet?
Ann Waldron and
Stephen Marchesi,
Grosset and Dunlap, 2009
Art Activity Pack:
Monet,
Mila Boutan,
Chronicle Books, 1996

Monet and Impressionists
for Kids,
Carol Sabbeth,
Cappella Books, 2002

Monet (Getting to Know
the World's Greatest
Artists),
Mike Venezia,
Lioncrest, 1995

Color your own
Monet Paintings,
Marty Noble,
Dover Publications, 2005
Colouring Book Monet,
Doris Kutschbach,
Prestel, 2006

Monet (Eyewitness Books),
Jude Welton,
Dorling Kindersley, 1999

Monet (Masterpieces:
Artists and Their Work),
Shelley Swanson Sateren,
Capstone Press, 2007

Art on the Wall:
Impressionism,
Jane Bingham,
Heinemann Library, 2008

Impressionism
(Art Revolutions),
Linda Bolton,
Belitha Press, 2003

Impressionism
(Eyewitness Guides),
Jude Welton,
1998

WEBSITES

giverny.org/monet/
welcome.htm

www.ibiblio.org/wm/
paint/auth/monet

www.expo-monet.com

www.intermonet.com

www.bbc.co.uk/history/
historic_figures/monet_
claude.shtml

www.nga.gov/collection/
gallery/gg85/gg85-
main1.html

www.claudemonet
gallery.org

www.bc.edu/bc_org/avp/
cas/fnart/art/monet1.html

http://claudemonet.org/

www.fondation-
monet.fr/uk/

www.wetcanvas.com/
Museum/Artists/m/Claude
_Monet/index.html

www.tate.org.uk/servlet/
ArtistWorks?cgroupid=
999999961&artistid=
1652&page=1

www.famouspainter.
com/claude.htm

www.nationalgallery.org.uk
/artists/claude-oscar-
monet

www.marmottan.com/
uk/claude_monet/
index.asp

www.claudemonet
works.com/about-
painter.aspx

www.moma.org/
explore/multimedia/
audios/1/7

www.visual-arts-
cork.com/famous-
artists/monet.htm

GLOSSARY

Abstract—Abstract art does not represent anything recognizable in the visible world. Abstract paintings can emphasize feelings, color, or shape, for instance, as artists focus on things other than what we see

Canvas—A heavy, closely woven fabric. Artists usually paint with oils on linen canvas, although cotton and hemp are also available. In Monet's day, canvas could be bought in standard sizes, stretched around a wooden frame and primed ready for use

Caricature—Normally means a picture of a person, usually a drawing, but can also mean a written or acted representation. Caricatures exaggerate characteristic features for comic effect

Cataracts—A cloudiness in the eye that some people experience as they age. It decreases vision and can eventually cause blindness.

Complementary colors—Colors that are directly opposite each other on the color wheel, such as red and green, blue and orange, and violet and yellow.

Composition—This word is often used as a general term meaning "painting," but the specific meaning refers to the combination or arrangement of elements in a picture

Conscripted—Compulsory (unavoidable) military service

Enveloppe—When Monet said he wanted to capture the *enveloppe*, he meant the air or atmosphere that surrounded whatever he was painting

Motif—A repeated theme in art, such as a subject, pattern, or idea

Pigment—This generally refers to a powder that is mixed with a liquid to make paint. The powder, usually made by grinding specific minerals or plants, is added to oils for oil painting but can be mixed with other mediums for different types of painting, such as tempera or watercolor

Tonality—Tonality refers to light and dark tones of a painting. In a painting, an artist has to create the correct tonality, from the darkest to the lightest – in color—to make it appear to have depth and to look realistic

INDEX

ACKNOWLEDGMENTS

Picture Credits t=top, b=bottom, c=center, l=left, r=right, OFC=outside front cover.

The Advertising Archive Ltd; 6tl. Photo © AKG London; 6cr. Art Institute of Chicago; 31tl, 31br. Art Institute of Chicago/Bridgeman Art Library, London; OFCb, 33t. © Bibliothèque Nationale of France, Paris; 8tl, 22cb. By permission of The British Library (7857dd,Opp80); 23t. Courtauld Institute Galleries, London. Photo © AKG London; 10/11cb. Enchanted Forest, 1947, Jackson Pollock © ARS, NY and DACS, London 1997 (Peggy Guggenheim Collection, Venice. Photo © AKG London); 35br. Improvisation 32 (Second Version), 1912, Wassily Kandinsky © ADAGP, Paris and DACS, London 1997 (Solomon R. Guggenheim, Museum, New York/Bridgeman Art Library, London); 34tr. Kunsthalle, Bremen/Lauros-Giraudon/Bridgeman Art Library, London; 32tl. Mary Evans Picture Library; 7tl, 7b, 14tl, 20bl, 24tl, 28bl, 30bl, 31tr. Metropolitan Museum of Art, New York/Bridgeman Art Library, London; 9tl & 12tl. Musee d'Art et d'Histoire, St. Denis, Paris/Giraudon/Bridgeman Art Library, London; 6bl. Musee du Louvre. Photo © AKG London; 8b. Musee d'Orsay, Paris. Photo © AKG London; 13tl, 16/17ct. Musee d'Orsay, Paris. Photo © AKG London/Erich Lessing; 10cl, 11tr, 13br, 14bl, 14br, 15cb & 36, 18tl, 20t, 21t, 26bl, 27bl, 29bl. Musee d'Orsay, Paris, France/Giraudon/Bridgeman Art Library, London; OFC (main image), OFCt, OFCc, 21b, 26/27ct. Musee de l'Orangerie, Paris/Lauros-Giraudon/Bridgeman Art Library, London; 28/29t & 34b. Musee Marmottan, Paris. Photo © AKG London; 19t. Musee Marmottan/Giraudon; 30tl. Reproduced by courtesy of the Trustees, The National Gallery, London; 24cl. National Gallery, London/Bridgeman Art Library, London; 25t. National Gallery of Art, Washington. Photo © AKG London; 16br. National Gallery of Scotland, Edinburgh/Bridgeman Art Library, London; 31cl & 34cr. Ny Carlsberg Glyptothek, Copenhagen. Photo © AKG London/Erich Lessing; 15tl. Phillips Collection, Washington DC/Bridgeman Art Library, London; 10tr. The Pierpoint Morgan Library/Art Resource, NY (S0109859); 32/33cb. Private Collection/Bridgeman Art Library, London; 12br. Pushkin Museum, Moscow/Bridgeman Art Library, London; 9cr. Roger Viollet/Frank Spooner Pictures; 9bl. Tate Gallery Archive; 34cl.

NOTE TO READERS

The website addresses are correct at the time of publishing. However, due to the ever-changing nature of the Internet, websites and content may change. Some websites can contain links that are unsuitable for children. The publisher is not responsible for changes in content or website addresses. We advise that Internet searches should be supervised by an adult.